THE RETREATS OF THOUGHT

Also by Kelly Cherry

POETRY
Hazard and Prospect: New and Selected Poems
Rising Venus
Death and Transfiguration
God's Loud Hand
Natural Theology
Relativity: A Point of View
Lovers and Agnostics

FICTION
We Can Still Be Friends
The Society of Friends
My Life and Dr. Joyce Brothers
The Lost Traveller's Dream
In the Wink of an Eye
Augusta Played
Sick and Full of Burning

NONFICTION
Girl in a Library: On Women Writers and the Writing Life
History, Passion, Freedom, Death, and Hope: Prose about Poetry
Writing the World
The Exiled Heart: A Meditative Autobiography

CHAPBOOKS/LIMITED EDITIONS
The Globe and the Brain, an essay
Welsh Table Talk, poems
An Other Woman, a poem
The Poem, an essay
Time out of Mind, poems
Benjamin John, a poem
Songs for a Soviet Composer, poems
Conversion, a story

TRANSLATION
Antigone, in *Sophocles*, ed. David R. Slavitt and Palmer Bovie, vol. 2
Octavia, in *Seneca, The Tragedies*, ed. David R. Slavitt, vol. 2

THE RETREATS
OF THOUGHT

poems

Kelly Cherry

Louisiana State University Press
Baton Rouge

Published by Louisiana State University Press
Copyright © 2009 by Kelly Cherry
All rights reserved
Manufactured in the United States of America
First printing

Designer: Michelle A. Neustrom
Typeface: Baskerville
Printer and binder: Thomson-Shore, Inc.

Library of Congress Cataloging-in-Publication Data

Cherry, Kelly.
  The retreats of thought : poems / Kelly Cherry.
    p. cm.
  ISBN 978-0-8071-3477-1 (alk. paper) — ISBN 978-0-8071-3478-8 (pbk. : alk. paper)
  I. Title.
  PS3553.H357R48 2009
  811'.54—dc22

                                                                    2009007540

The author wishes to thank the editors and staff of the publications in which some of the poems in this book first appeared, sometimes under different titles or in different versions: *America:* "What, Then?"; *Atlantic Review:* "To a Fellow Graduate Student," "The Truth," "Apologia Pro Vita Sua"; *CutThroat:* "Deceived," "The Contagion of Grief"; *Harvard Review:* "Chance in a Universe of Values"; *Idaho Review:* "A Throw of the Dice," "Time," "Where Is the Past?" "The Varieties of Religious Experience," "Matter," "What Matters"; *Image:* "On Value," "The Community of Minds"; *Iris:* "My Mother, Dying"; *Iron Horse Review:* "That Contradicting the Law of Contradiction Does Not Have to Entail Mysticism," "The Mind-Body Problem"; *Literature and Belief:* "On a Seldom If Ever Remarked and Difficult but Rewarding Application of Forgiveness"; *Per Contra:* "Aspects of the Novel"; *Pivot:* "Space," "On the Extreme Paltriness of What We Can Know," "Running to Beat the Clock," "The Special Theory of Relativity," "How to Write a Sonnet"; *Poetry:* "On the Work Ethic" (July, 2002); *Southern Poetry Review:* "Self-Consciousness"; *Southern Review:* "String Theory"; *When She Named Fire: An Anthology of Contemporary Poetry by American Women,* ed. Andrea Hollander Budy (Autumn House Press, 2008): "Truth and Tolerance," "Fair Is Fair: A Dialogue between Husband and Wife," "On the Soul."

The paper in this book meets the guidelines for permanence and durability of the Committee on Production Guidelines for Book Longevity of the Council on Library Resources. ∞

To the College of Liberal Arts
at the University of Alabama in Huntsville

for the support, interest, and intellectual climate
that made these poems possible

. . .in our subject you will find
How one thing leads on to the next in order,
And wind your way toward the retreats of thought
To drag the truth from hiding.

—LUCRETIUS, *De Rerum Natura,* trans.
Palmer Bovie, 1.405–8

Contents

THE RETREATS OF THOUGHT

Proem

Beginning with ontology and moving
to philosophy of mind (what is the self?
how can we know the world, and does proving
a thing make it truer than the Delph-
ic Oracle's pronouncements?), through political
philosophy, ethics, and aesthetics,
this little volume is in search of all
the truth that it can find this side of the Styx.
Examining retreats of thought, where truth
is wont to hide, it tries to shine a light
and, frankly, in consequence can be uncouth,
but that, too, is a philosophical plight,
and sometimes it is couth enough to thank
those who tried to cruise the Styx and sank.

A Throw of the Dice

At any rate, I am convinced that *He* does not play dice.

—ALBERT EINSTEIN, Letter to Max Born, 4 December 1926

The question that confronts us first is, Why
something? Why is there anything at all
instead of simply nothing, nada? I
suggest that something is more probable
than nothing—that of which there can't be more
than one at most—while on the other hand
abound glad possibilities galore
for life and stuff. Please don't misunderstand.
I can't concur with that favorite reply
of priests: "The odds against our universe
existing are so infinitely high
we must believe in God." The odds aren't worse
than for any other ordered universe.
If there's a God, He does not throw *loaded* dice.

Space

We pretty much agree that it exists
but *where* does it exist? Everywhere
(except beyond the roomy span of prayer
or that last best hope of a human tryst,
the finite, bounded, spreading universe)?

Or should we look, instead, within the mind,
the bounded universe's double bind,
where things that go wrong will always get worse,
for something Kant contends is *a priori*?

(What if he had envisioned space a womb
in which thought, conceived, would in time assume
the shape of that which it will come to be . . .)

Not neither here nor there, it is the place
birthed into being by Original Grace.

Time

From that therefore, which is not yet, through that, which hath no
space, into that, which now is not.
—AUGUSTINE, *Confessions*, Book XI, trans. Edward B. Pusey

Augustine thought that time unlocked the door
of the future, rushing into the present
and then the past, though it's my metaphor,
that vacated house, not his, whence went
time in such a hurry it barely brushed
the here and now, perhaps nicking a corner
or knocking off a hat that then got crushed
beneath a bus, a chill like a coroner
in its wake, a coroner with a cold,
his face as blue as any in his morgue,
where he dices some stiff whose run's been cancelled
by an untoward event that seemed as rogue
as a rogue elephant or Errol Flynn,
but no, it was time's way the dead was in.

Where Is the Past?

Wheresoever then is whatsoever is, it is only as present.
    —AUGUSTINE, *The Confessions,* Book XI, trans. Edward B. Pusey

Augustine said the only time is now.
The past is merely memory, although
by memory we also mean history.
What of the past lost to the mystery
of forgetfulness, the bits and pieces
fallen like unheard trees, unthought theses,
out of mind and into nonexistence?
Suppose whole chunks have broken loose, a tense
like an asteroid belt, ranging, and out
of control, something one certainly ought
to steer around if it were there, but it
is not, is it? At least it is not quite.
Where does the time go? Ah. It goes with us
as we step to the front and off the bus.

Running to Beat the Clock

Time stretches out before us—and behind—
as far as we can see, the light of stars
a window onto time that's out of mind.
Are they the lightning bugs God trapped in jars,
fire flickering to dark? Was there a God
who wound a clock, said prayers, went to sleep,
Supreme Deity snoozing in the land of Nod?
He is not likely to be counting sheep,
which is to say, ourselves, we humans who
must run to beat the clock because the yard
of time it measures shrinks, like sodden wool,
to next to nothing, something strayed and downward
of anything, our future and our past
both relatively brief and going fast.

The Special Theory of Relativity

There's no such thing as unenacted time:
time is theater, an effect whose cause
is one of physics' fundamental laws:
the body's movement is a pantomime
of point of view. You know the paradigm:
a man who's riding on a beam of light
will seem to disappear into the night—
sort of like a sentence distracted by rhyme—
lost to his friends, for whom the years revolve
around mundane matters of love and marriage,
children, the deaths of pets and parents, work:
instead of beams of light, they know the dark
returning and returning, feel their age,
recall this life before it began to evolve.

String Theory

My father played the violin and taught
music theory—a theory of the string,
if not string theory, that equation sought
by those who'd like a Theory of Everything.
He read the new quartets—Diamond, Riegger,
Carter, Piston—as soon as they appeared,
scores of scores: an impassioned man eager
for harmonies that had not yet been heard,
for music must be made within the mind
first and only after sounded. "World sheet"
is what they call the surface of the kind
of curve that vibrates to the rhythmic beat
of relativity. My father knew
a string quartet is more than two plus two.

A Stillness So Pure It Cannot Be Perceived

Begin here: space and time are relative,
and one does not exist without the other.
Thus place is what a moment has to have
to happen, and nothing happens nowhere.
Thus time is movement and eternity
stillness so pure it cannot be perceived
(as may be said also of God's pity,
unless it really is to be believed
that he so loved the world he gave to it
his only begotten son, that they should live
who him receive). Can mere mind intuit
a That to Which the way is negative?
Always, questions. I tried to clear my head
and think, but sometimes I gave up and read.

Matter

Has extension, density; can be felt:
the fall of scarf across your chilled shoulders;
the unforgiving floor on which you knelt
while weeping; dear body of love that molders
in the mute grave, despite your desperate tears.
The stars burn on like lost love, which smolders
in the heart's hearth for a while, but even stars
go out; the cosmos grows older and colder,
for substance changes form and in the process
reveals that it was never anything more
than hope and memory, the defeating farthest
distance being that which is at the core
of everything, the brute, unfathomable reaches
of space that matter, brave as soldiers, breaches.

What Matters

What's matter but the stuff that takes up space:
a definition that will surely do
even for one who'd build an airtight case,
such as Hamlet judging his flesh too . . . too . . .
"sullied," some say, but let us say "solid,"
although, again, you know, it hardly matters.
Even the most crowded, vile, and squalid
den, compacted of addicts, outlaws, and squatters,
contains a whole unsettled, free frontier.
The body cartographs a world within,
oceans between tiny bones of the ear,
unconnected islands construed as skin,
and all that is, is so filled up with space,
we must be light and floating, fixed in place.

That the Sense of Being Here Is Unmediated and Is a Source of the Sense of Self

"Hereness" cannot refer to a mediated web of "heres" exactly because the individual "here" is established by being *out of* mediated relation.

—BRIAN MARTINE, professor of philosophy at the University of Alabama in Huntsville, from a manuscript in progress titled "Where Are the Philosophers Now?"

The moment I suppose that I am here
I know I am not there—nor there—nor there,
nowhere but here, in fact, though here is there
from another point of view. Do I not hear
my heart, my greedy breaths? Come close. You'll hear
the me I am. As for the others, they're
elsewhere, and never any nearer than there.
It's so lonely being the only one here.
The world resists my charm. You might reply
that "world" includes me. Well, it does, except
when I regard it, then it's other than
myself, a thing apart. Hard though I try,
it's I who, longing for oneness, disrupt
the flow of the unmediated one.

Consciousness

Must consciousness be prepositional,
be "of" some thing (however loosely "thing"
may be defined), be situational?
Or is it independent of any thing,
Platonic form the world itself might long
to emulate, as though the thought *to sing*
existed in the being of the song
you hum while thinking of everything
you meant to get right that you got so wrong?
Perhaps the music of the spheres is heard
only by those who think meaning may hang
upon the uses of a single word
like "consciousness." Or maybe not. Perhaps
celestial music is sensation and synapse.

My Mother, Dying

My mother, like my father, was a musician (a violinist). —K. C.

Unconscious, says the doctor, speaking of
his patient who has slipped into a coma,
your dying mother, whom you surely love
despite your scars, your open wounds, the trauma
of never being who she wished that she
had been and wanted you to be for her,
but who was that if not nearly every
strong, spirited, legendary daughter
who ever lived and spoke to her from myth
or history, Athena, Aphrodite,
Curie, radium like a river of death
through her whole body, that work-wracked body,
St. Joan of Arc, or Jacqueline du Pré.

"You're freed to write," someone would later say.

Such rank ignorance! On such brash display!

On the Extreme Paltriness of
What We Can Know

The world as it appears may also be
the sum of what there is but probably
not, since alternatives are infinite.

Yet equal opportunity obtains
between the one and many, doesn't it. . . .
A thinker, reconsidering, refrains
from placing bets on whether noumena
outnumber phenomena.
                So much remains
unknown, and even studious Meno,
whom Socrates conducted on the trains
of thought, might want to add *unknowable*,
for if the nature of our puny brains
is such that we're inherently unable
to outwit ourselves, confusion reigns
(meaning that man does indeed live in chains).

What Is Man?

So what *are* we? Experience, I'd say.
Not *what* we experience: experience
itself. It's what we mean by "sentience,"
this being that we do every day
of our lives. Useless, Skinner, to inveigh
against the fact: it is *social* science,
with ourselves as the irrefutable evidence
that life is feeling, how ever and any way,
but something all the time. We testify
that something happens to us. What we do
in response is not adult or child's play
but the work of living. When we die,
experience is the one thing we take to
the grave, the estate we cannot give away
(although art tries). Death is hell to pay.

Self-Consciousness

I know myself as self, and furthermore,
know that this self will not persist forever,
although it seems to me it has a core
that continues like a low-grade fever
through all the hours of my shortening days,
an illness, and a diagnosable one
despite the deconstructionist who says
whatever we think we are, we are no one,
that anything we do can be undone,
including the construction of a self,
that as a writer I should know my ruin
cannot be shored against by a bookshelf,
and maybe this is true, though I'd have sworn
my self was me the second I was born.

There Is No Higher Consciousness

There is no higher consciousness that rules
us, neither spiritual force nor physical person;
no karmic justice whose stringency schools
us in the moral purposes of reason.
No man has ever risen like the sun,
erasing the shadow of mortality,
or compensated for the cost of sin,
death and despair. No mutuality
exists between good and evil, duty
and disaster, or sacrifice and self.
Whatever may be thought sublimest beauty
is beautiful, but beauty's not enough,
for it merely exists. Art may inspire;
it can't uplift the dead one whit higher.

What, Then?

"Do unto others as you'd be done unto."
Of course, it's not so simple: needed are
imagination; willingness to give;
according to the great Socratic directive,
the knowledge of just who it is you are;
and courage, for how else can we be true

to what goodness demands that we believe:
that the kingdom of God that is within
is but the place from which we must begin,
as if we all are waiting to receive
the gift that everyone, like a magus,
must bear, by light of some guiding star,
across a perilous distance, close or far,
a sense of what it's like, being us.

To Descartes, On the Method

René Descartes was stationed in Neuberg, Germany, with the
Bavarian army of Frederick V, when, on November 10, 1619,
he envisioned a new method of doing philosophy, arguing that
reason must be based on clear and distinct ideas, such as *cogito,
ergo sum* ("Je pense donc je suis"). It was Blaise Pascal who noted
that "the heart has its reasons, which the mind knows not."

"I think, therefore I am," but nowadays
certain theorists might question if that "you"
is not a socially constructed Who,
linguistic figment, or hormonal phase.
"It's like putting the horse before Descartes,"
someone might say—for all I know, has said—
although anyone who's actually read
your reasoning will hear her Pascalian heart
beat harder as she thinks of you "alone
in a stove-heated room," sweeping away
all thoughts that are unclear and indistinct
(but are they only incompletely known?),
bold as a German general that day,
so ironic and Gallically succinct.

The Mind-Body Problem

The most precise presentation of the mind-body problem, central to western philosophy, is found in the work of Descartes and often referred to as Cartesian dualism.

Imagine body without mind? A zombie.
(It's animate but hardly animated.)
The mind without body is Abercrombie
minus Fitch, the two incorporated,
or anyway the one; and married, though
the marriage was arranged. They'd never dated;
the eager mind was not allowed to know
a thing until parents negotiated.
Now mind sleeps in. Body's an early riser
(as zombies are), easily stimulated
though requiring a pencil with eraser
to do the Sunday crossword, caffeinated
and chewing on the pencil, and the mind-
body problem's a puzzle of a kind.

Deceived

Descartes argued that because God is good we
are not deceived in our impressions.

Epiphenomena—concomitant
but meaningless—is how some thinkers view
emotions: stuff that like a sycophant
somehow manages to latch onto you,
is always there, trying to make you feel
that you are what everything is all
about, you are both the hub and big wheel,
the world is the Response but you the Call,
it's about you, and why shouldn't it be?
You feel so much. Surely no one has ever
known such a broad array of affect so deeply,
or otherwise, our life is a fever
that consumes us, and we toss and turn,
delirious, as our deceived hearts burn.

Sex

Friction; transference of bodily fluid:
there is nothing immaterial in
any of this, nothing spritely or druid
about us, nothing angelic, saintly, or zen.
I pant; you pant; our arms and legs entwine
as if we mean to yoke ourselves together.
That leg behind your back, isn't it mine?
Oh, about sex there is nothing ether-
eal, it's grinding hipbones and pumping elbows,
it's a foot in the face, the dizzy kiss
that can't remember what part of the body it goes
on, and who cares if the laggard mind might miss
out, or construe the nipple as a rose?
Almost, you'd trade philosophy for this.

Aspects of the Poem

We have defined a story as a narrative of events arranged
in their time-sequence. A plot is also a narrative of events,
the emphasis falling on causality.

    —E. M. FORSTER, *Aspects of the Novel*

Hume proved conclusively we cannot know
if anything is caused by something else.
In other words, our narrative has no
plot, is a patched physique that lacks a pulse.
Well, *there's* a plot of sorts, and history
is buried there, the one thing coming after
another, but it's still a mystery
to me as well as to Mr. E. M. Forster
why it is that this has followed that
and not this or *that*. The novelist
cannot accept that things occur without
cause, or thinks that if they do, at least
they shouldn't in his book; wherefore, I say,
if God exists, He prefers poetry.

Free Will

Responsibility is the concern
here, for how can we be held liable
for actions we've not caused? It's not viable
to say that what we get we never earn;
a fact of life that each of us must learn
is that the notion of fate is a fable,
grand but flawed, or else we are not able
to make moral distinctions, say the turn

that someone did you was a good one, or
was not—and are your deeds impervious
to judgment? No. Comeuppance is a part
of being human (as, of course, is error).
And yet how fateful and how fabulous
is the irresponsible, willful heart.

The Examined Life

Some days it does feel rather like a test.
You've crammed and thought and crammed and thought and still
you know only that failure is the best
that you can hope to do, so if free will
exists, why don't you walk out of the room
right now? And where's the teacher, anyway?
You thought you'd pass? What else did you assume?
(What sneaky presuppositions have been in play?)
For starters, that to live a life worth living
you must be able to say something about
it, something true and therefore worth believing.
Ergo, the one thing *you* could never doubt
was that the writing of serious poetry
means making art of thought. Q. E. D.

Chance in a Universe of Values

We love the pleasures of surprise, grow cold
as corpses at the thought of accident.
The pleasures of surprise are manifold,
but unanticipated tragedy
negates the meaning of all that we meant
to do and be. That thing you did or said,
what would you not give now to take it back?
Each life's a train that will run off a track
and this is also true of history,
which is the long aftermath of a wreck,
the landscape strewn with bodies of the dead.
To understand this, it helps, I find, to read
a book titled *Values in a Universe
of Chance: Selected Essays of Charles S. Peirce.*

A Pause

A pause here, while I grieve for unfulfilled
intention, work I thought that I would do
but set aside, moving it to the margins
of my life. For ideas unexamined,
implications left languishing, a field
ununified. . . . I did not adumbrate
the metaphysics of Charles Sanders Peirce,
compose a treatise on time, or justify
the ways of God to man, or man to God,
or the ways of one woman to herself, and yet
I cherish the days and nights I read the works
of minds attuned to thoughts lofty and precise.
I turned the page, refilled my coffee cup,
and gave myself up to unmatched pleasure.

To a Fellow Graduate Student

*For James Cargile, now professor and director of Colloquium Series
in the Philosophy Department of The University of Virginia*

My first year at The University
of Virginia, we shared an office in
Cabell Hall, though you were ahead of me.
I watched with awe as you uncapped your pen,
pulled your feet from desktop to floor and sat
up straight to write in ink on unlined paper,
recap, lean back, put feet back up and wait
to see if the next thought, too, would be a keeper.
In my eyes, you were W. V. O. Quine's
equal, proof being your desk, completely clear
except for that one sheet of abstruse signs.
Mine was strewn with books, an unlit bonfire
of sanctioned texts and illicit poetry.

You taught me to believe in what I thought.

On Value

The graduate philosophy department at The University
of Virginia emphasized analytic philosophy.

In Charlottesville, at twenty-one, I was
assigned to write a paper on value:
What is value? Something that something has,
a property? Product of a point of view?
A measurement, perhaps, or function of—
what? I was working on a Ph.D.
I had long hair. We value what we love,
I thought (minutes before love became free).
My bangs fell to my eyes. I was sitting
at a small Formica table, legal pad
in hand, when it struck me I'd be quitting
school soon. I love philosophy but had,
I saw, no way within the practice of it
to say I value it because I love it.

The Problem of Meaning

Briefly, then: I think nothing has meaning.
What is, is as it is, and yes, it has,
of course, ramifications, thus seeming
to take on grave significance in the as-
sociation with whatever else is,
although significance is not the same
as meaning, but assumes a hidden premise:
that what is meaningful is so for some-
one, meaning meaning is a kind of value,
and is that argument not circular,
making meaning what we attribute to
the meaningful, while the unblinking star
that gazes down on us without concern
observes our problematic planet turn?

A Brief Review of What We Have
Covered So Far

I think that something and nothing are one
thing, the moon with one side bright as joy,
the other dark, unshined on by the sun
and cold as January in Sheboy-
gan. I think creation and consciousness
are the same one side of a Moebius strip,
unending, so that each is more or less
the other. I think time is a round trip,
a journey sweet but often hard and lonely
and taken on the train of thought from here
to here, that all times happen at once, only
past, present, future are how they appear.
I think that when we die we die for good
and ever, making room in the neighborhood.

The Varieties of Religious Experience

To be is to become. There is no state
of being that is not provisional,
as transient as weather, spring or fall;
none not blurred, befogged, and intermediate,
or none that's actual. Plato's postulate,
a realm of forms both static and ideal,
would make the abstract realer than the real,
esteem a noun above its predicate,

and some believe in a reality
that lives forever, will be and has been,
remains with us now, and never alters,
is incorruptible, but we agree
that faith's the evidence of things not seen,

explaining the variety of altars.

On the Soul

By *soul* I mean the self described by passion,
for passion shapes us. We are carved and hollowed
by what we love—love irrationally,
perhaps, and yet we think our hearts hallowed
by love that acquaints us with the contours of
ourselves, until we know ourselves as well
as the arms and legs and back and knees of love,
the body of it, sweat and salt and smell.
The love of thought is as identifying
as any other passion and survives
time's despoliation—love undying,
for as long as the sense of one's self lives,
and then the soul departs, leaving behind
the record of an open, responsive mind.

The Problem of Pain

Regarding the afflictions of our people
and not forgetting how the birds and beasts
suffer, under a zealous desert sun
or the whiplash winds of driving winter,
we ask how we can call creation good
that mandates loss and sorrow, that permits,
indeed, requires, of all who live, a measure
not only of felt pain, physical or
mental, but also the causing of the same
to others so that anguish must recount
its tale endlessly, like the number π,
a wife who has been left, a veteran
of a forgotten war, autistic child,
or wallpaper, the infinite blue sky.

The Contagion of Grief
A Note on the Preceding Poem

And yes, we are the cause of suffering
and cannot not be, and cannot provide
immunity against ourselves, Bufferin
or anodyne: someday we shall have died,
and even if we lived a perfect life
(especially if we did) somebody cried.
There is no way that this contagion of grief
might be contained except to spread such pain
that when we die, our death will bring relief.
It is this paradox that is the bane
of our existence. Those who think Christ rose
from death that we might not have lived in vain
vaccinate themselves with a potent dose
of loss against all that we have to lose.

Good and Evil

Can good and evil be defined by absence
of each other?

        Let's say that good is light
without shadow, as hard to see as night,
a sun best viewed through indirection, lens
devised to let us look up by looking down.

If evil is the lack of good, a hole
in the heart as black as a hole in space, a hell
that blinds us so we do not see our own
selves—the shadows we throw, living our lives—
it is invisible, a place we fall
into forever.

        In light of this, perhaps
we see but darkly that we might surmise
even the Absolute is not the All
for here we are, mortals in moral eclipse.

In Suffering Is No Deliverance nor Instruction but There Is an Opportunity

In suffering is no deliverance nor
instruction, or if something's to be learned,
it could as well be envy, ethnic war,
or bitterness (what's left when all has burned
to ashes, bone that glares amid the heap,
identifying tooth that asks a tooth
in trade). We weep. I do not think we weep
to save ourselves or testify to truth,
but opportunity is where you find
it, and in tribulation we may discover
a chance to turn the cheek, be strong and kind,
the sum of suffering the world over
lessened thereby. (But even those who don't
now suffer could be kinder were they wont.)

On a Seldom If Ever Remarked and Difficult but Rewarding Application of Forgiveness

We can forgive the ignorant, who know
not what they do, and maybe we'll forgive
the evil, who know what they do but not how
to love and consequently not how to live,
but what about the very fortunate,
those noticeable men and women whose lucky stars
shine like Broadway marquees? Their enviable fate—
that talent! those white teeth! the Pulitzers!—
decenters us: at last we recognize
that we are not the be-all and the end-
all and not even the apple of all eyes
and while we know the worth of books we've signed
we're grateful for the wider view given
us by those whose gifts we have forgiven.

First Reply to Plato

In Book X of *The Republic* Plato argues that poets and poetry are,
for the most part, to be exiled from the "well-ordered" State, be-
cause they do not tell the truth and encourage emotionalism.

No, no, no. The philosophers
and poets will be neighbors, and the kings
will be dethroned, demoted to mere gofers.
That will go some way toward improving things.

Kings running errands for philosophers
will be a just and righteous revolution
but we shall also revolutionize verse,
decree philosopher and poet one
and the very same. These poet-philosophers,
enacting legislation protecting beauty
and truth and seeing themselves for once as movers
and shakers, will gladly do their civic duty
and, whenever they convene the senate,
pledge allegiance to the sonnet.

Second Reply to Plato

No, no, no. Poets must be welcome
to share a backyard fence with philosophers
and, over it, discuss the joys of home-
owning. Indeed, since both tend to be loafers,
shooting the breeze with no thought for the time,
they probably should just move in together,
the card above their doorbell reading *Rhyme*
and *Reason*. They'll be more than fair-weather
friends, though that is none of government's business.
That business is kings: what shall we do
with all the kings? Behead them, more or less.
For justice to be done, we must undo
injustice. Let us crown a philosopher-*poet*
as our head of state. Surely that will do it.

Fair Is Fair

A Dialogue between Husband and Wife

I was incensed. "Even if it's true
that the best things in life are free, there are not
enough of them. Or else some damn idiot
got a good deal more than any fool is due.
Meanwhile, the poor cannot afford to sue
congress for a chicken in every pot.
Justice? I guess it's *just* that hell is hot.
In death the rich can live on Supply Side Stew."

My gentle husband said, "Suppose justice
isn't a balancing of scales, an equation
between terms, but rather a singular gorgeous thing
to be weighed against sheerest emptiness?"

"Plato's metaphysics is out of fashion."

"So what?" he said. "Has the North Star stopped shining?"

On the Work Ethic

Max Weber, German sociologist and economist, is best known as the
author of *The Protestant Ethic and the Spirit of Capitalism*, in which he
describes the relation of the Calvinist work ethic to the development
of capitalist societies.

"Christmas gift": I was born on the twenty-first of December. —K. C.

It's not so much that you subscribe to it
as that you were enlisted in its rolls
from birth and knew you must find work and do it
as soon as you had finished playing dolls
(although you still think wistfully of the one
with true blue eyes and thick, black eyelashes
who'd wet her gown and cry until the moon
turned off its light and left the window sashes
to shiver through a night of wind and snow.
Your doll was fast asleep now, dreaming of
places she'd like, when she grew up, to go
in Santa's merry sleigh, which had paused on the roof
of this shabby tenement long enough to leave
you the Christmas gift of a child to love).

A Flaw in the Argument from Design Not Previously Pointed Out, Although Many Flaws Have Been Pointed Out

We do not even know whether we are
created, and the splendor of our star,

the sun, our moon, the blue-and-green *dreydl*
of our planet (humankind's scenic cradle)

may tell us more about our mind's-eyes than
about cosmic purpose, blueprint, or plan:

because we feel a child's love for a parent,
we think it inarguably apparent

that the gracious hand of God is guiding
us— but why would He point to Himself in hiding

behind the beauty of our universe,

O Syllogism behind the scrim of verse,

unless, of course, beauty *is* truth, or all
the truth we need to know, after the Fall?

The Phenomenology of Beauty

Such a lot of beauty is incidental,
the composition fortuitous and fleeting,
the moment so individual
describing it is almost like cheating
because description is a sleight of hand
that stacks particulars in categories,
the Ding an sich *a sort of analysand*
for analytic thinkers . . . .
                    A poet worries
about this, wanting to incorporate,
in art that lasts, the vagrant, moving truth,
which is at once translucent and opaque.
She hopes to be as devoted as Ruth,
seeing the poet's inescapable duty
as the timeless pursuit of truth and beauty.

The Pursuit of Beauty and Truth

> Mathematics is intensely beautiful, but still the connection between
> mathematics and beauty baffles me. Mathematicians pursue under-
> standing, not beauty.
>
> —BARRY MAZUR, mathematician, quoted in *Harvard Magazine*
> (with apologies: Mazur is also a poet, and perhaps I have taken
> the quotation out of context)

But understanding, Barry, is the aim
of artists as it is of mathematicians.
Our legacy of Rubenses and Titians
derives from thinkers searching for the same
quarry you seek, the necessary game.
Perhaps you think that artists are beauticians,
obsessed with surfaces, that musicians
soothe savage breasts because they want to tame
the wild, blowing truth your colleagues pursue.
If that's the case, you need to learn the language
of art (syntactic relation of viewer to view);
how composers (even the chancy Cage)
explore time; and that, to understand *you*,
a pissed-off poet scribbles on a page.

Snow Globe for Ian Hacking

Ian Hacking is now University Professor Emeritus at the University
of Toronto and Emeritus Professor at the Collège de France. He
teaches widely and is the author of many highly regarded books
on logic, epistemology, philosophy of mind, and the conceptual
history of science.

It's gone now, every single thing I learned
in Mathematical Logic, in Cabell Hall,
and yet I aced the final and the class,
and loved even the hard and thorny parts
(the math guys caught on quick; the rest of us
were wannabe philosophers, and found
the going rough at first, to say the least).
I ask you, where has all that learning gone?
I still remember how you started on one
blackboard and worked your way around the room,
four walls whited-out in a blizzard of chalk.
Oh, it was blinding!—the beauty of Gödel's Proof.

Like gazing into someone's mind and seeing
his thoughts, no two alike, come into being.

How to Write a Sonnet

You may count syllables but must count feet,
and they, of course, may number more or fewer
depending on the way you hear the beat.
Like mortal love, scansion is impure,
which means mathematics is not enough,
you have to trust your ear, and this is true
again when sounding out a rhyme. It's tough
to write a sonnet, though there are one or two
things harder, such as giving birth, or dying.
(Poets who claim they're pregnant with conception
are full of bunk and more or less lying,
less to the degree they practice self-deception.)
The most important thing about the sonnet
is whether truth is to be found in it.

What Is Truth?

A concept without meaning, many say,
dismissing it because they have been taught
that truth is something like a noun manqué
instead of something struggled for or sought.
Abstract a concept from a predicate,
they say, and what you get is funny money,
no good for paying for the meal you ate
this morning, even if the eggs *were* runny.
We may assert of something that it's true
but not that it's the truth, nor does it follow
truth's anything other than a term of value.
Language is not the firelight but the hollow
in which we live, and what light comes to us
is as silent as it is luminous.

The Community of Minds

Charles Sanders Peirce, American philosopher, was born
in 1839 and died in 1914.

[T]hought is what it is, only by virtue of its addressing a
future thought which is in its value as thought identical
with it, though more developed. In this way, the existence
of thought now depends on what is to be hereafter; so
that it has only a potential existence, dependent on the
future thought of the community. . . . Accordingly, just
as we say that a body is in motion, and not that motion is
in a body, we ought to say that we are in thought and not
that thoughts are in us.
—"Some Consequences of Four Incapacities"

Can it be that truth is easily frightened
and shies from us? Or have we not yet looked
sufficiently around our sun-brightened
haven, because it's we who have been spooked
by shadows on the wall—and they our own,
perhaps, or possibly not, but if not
they can only be the shadows thrown
by that upon which shines the same fond light
that shines on us. Within this shining space,
we also glimpse one another: I see
the daylight gathered in your waking face
as if it were a gift you give to me,
your view of things expanding our shared world,
the universe expanding from the word.

Truth and Tolerance

"As there's no truth, or none that we can know,
we must be tolerant of one another."
This is how the argument should go,
according to today's philosopher
or literary theorist. One might reply,
"Without belief in truth, the concept of
tolerance is meaningless. Anarchy
does not work well as a substitute for love,
and who can love who does not think she knows
a reason for the choices that she makes?
Or must she love the worm that sickens the rose
with its own secret love?" William Blake's
dark apostrophe to a dying rose:
so true and tolerant her tired heart aches.

The Difference between Talent and Genius

Talent scores a bull's-eye others miss
but genius nails a target no one sees,
said Schopenhauer. Talent's a narcissist
(let's add), but genius turns its back and flees
into the world, wishing to educate
itself in reality. Whereas talent
demands to be adored, acclaimed as "great"
(no matter it demurs), thought heaven-sent
(fulfilling fantasies of specialness),
genius endures rejection for the sake
of something not itself, which it is less
than and respects and loves. We ought to take
genius as an example of altruism,
less light than prism.

Greatness in Art

To tell the truth, what else. And find it first
(the railway journey to Marabar, archetypal
sea-hunt or Alpine quarantine, the quest
for the Holy Grail, innocent Parsifal
in armor, sweltering and sweet), although
what lies between the truth and us is us.
It's we that we must find a way to go
beyond. It's we who are deadly dangerous,
and so seductive, leading ourselves on
toward a false idea of success,
for art may be a kind of Armageddon,
a universal struggle, a moral contest,
but the heroic distance we have to span
is that between the self and the human.

To Tell the Truth

It's what you think you know (if truth be told).
Or what you do not know but wish you did,
or think you wish you did but for the cold
hard truth of the matter, which is that you lied,
you fear it's what you thought would be the case.
In fact, you fancy the filigree of falsehood,
the way a lie can trim the truth like lace,
the way it bends truth to the common good.
You like the fiction, the nervy swerve of it,
the way it will sweeten a bitter pill.
In sum, you think everyone could profit
by speaking at least somewhat better of the ill.
To keep the peace, you would choose consequences
over truth's unvarnished sentences.

Talking Back to Wittgenstein

In his *Tractatus-Logico Philosophicus,* Austrian philosopher
Ludwig Wittgenstein (1889–1951) proposed criteria for
"meaningful" language, mandating the exclusion from
philosophical inquiry of other kinds of discourse. He
cautioned us: "Whereof one cannot speak, thereof one
must be silent."

"Whereof one cannot speak," let us present,
in something like a bounded universe,
the untold truth (untold but omnipresent)
as shape and symbol: music, painting, verse.
In this way, art says more than language can.
In art, we carry on a dialogue
with silence, thereby learning how to listen.
I will say, knowing it is not the vogue
to say it, that art comprises language and silence,
containing both within a field of thought.
Art is a function of intelligence,
therefore, and teaches what cannot be taught
any other way, that where we're mute,
art may analyze, agree, confute.

Apologia Pro Vita Sua

I had questions. I also thought I knew
an answer, which there was no way to state,
alas. The truth to which I would be true
could only be embodied, made incarnate,
because the Word occurs within Being
and not the other way around, language
enacted by the mind that makes it, something
beyond and prior to the turning page.
Thus art transcends philosophy, and thus
the artist surrenders her allotted days
to the one artistic aim that is serious:
to present what we can never paraphrase.
Reading herself, the agnostic poet prays,
Mea culpa, mea culpa, deus.

That Contradicting the Law of Contradiction
Does Not Have to Entail Mysticism

The question was, To be or not to be?
and logic teaches us that we must choose,
that it is not the case that B can be
both B and not B, but the latest news
from the scientific front now suggests
what art has always known: that comedy
is divine and that God, like Yorick, jests.
Think of *viruses* or *light:* how each may be
its formal opposite. I do not say
that opposites must fade and blur to one
but that truth is contrary, like a play
by William Shakespeare (or a poem by Donne)
that in the end shows us how our philo-
sophical notions revert *ad nihilo.*

The Truth

Thales of Miletus, for whom the First Principle was water, specu-
lated that the earth is an island floating on the river from which
it solidified. Thales achieved distinction in many areas, including
astronomy. In *Theaetetus*, Socrates tells us that Thales fell into a well
while gazing at the stars.

It's what we wanted not to have to face:
no, not the image waiting in the mirror
but absence of oneself, the much sheerer
horror of disappearing without a trace,
of everyone disappearing like that—
poof, and then they're gone, candles blown out
on a birthday, life a general rout,
and now the earth could just as well be flat
as round, support an atmosphere or not,
be cooled, like thoughtful Thales, by oceanic
currents that are never harsh or manic
but temperate as reason, or be hot
as hell, which is the place we'd think we were
should we behold all who have gone from here.

Regarding Our Children

Think now of magnitude and distance, stars
surrounded by a darkness thick as fur
although unfelt. You think we'll get to Mars?
A baby step. I wonder if we'll ever
discover the edge of the edgeless universe.
Our minds demand of us an understanding
of who and where we are, knowledge of first
and last things, a sense that, as we're handing
our places to a younger generation,
we leave a legacy of useful fact.
Unluckily for them, we know but a fraction
of the whole—and comprehend still less, at that.
We travel into darkness. Our children
enter a world beyond their forebears' ken.

A Theory of Everything

No drama of dualism, nor scheme
in which the many handily resolve
to one, nor inspired poet's pipe dream
a hapless visitor from Porlock could dissolve
with a knock on the door, and not the Platonic form
of something (floating, disembodied, outside
time but imitated by a norm
that is never *videlicet* but only *vide*),
truth is existence, and existence is
itself and not-self and so it cannot hide
anywhere, while we, among existence's
thin gaps and folds, are scattered far and wide,
adrift and hidden, crying *adieu, adieu,*
as our horizon vanishes from view.

A Final Reflection

"[T]he Ghost in the Machine," from *The Concept of Mind* by
Gilbert Ryle (1900–1976), one of the most influential books
in contemporary philosophy. In it, Ryle argues against the
Cartesian dichotomy of mind and body.

How quiet the night, as if you had been lost
in thought and now looked up to see a ghost.
Your hand goes to your cheek, where something cold
has touched it. Oh, what is it that you hold?

A cobweb, as if it were the specter's spoor.
And what was that? Did someone slam a door?
Is someone there? Speak up!

         Don't be afraid.
Your light has not yet darkened into shade.

This cobweb clinging to my fingertips . . .
Can I have clasped the shadow of a wisp,
echo of an echo? I thought I felt
the tremor from a long-forgotten fault;
it shook me to my core.

         Don't be afraid.
That was only the ghost your own mind made.

Postscript

I cannot say exactly what compelled me
to assemble my thoughts on the noble subject
of philosophy, but I can say they held me
in their mariner thrall until at last I wrecked
upon cave-riddled shores where truth abides.
I salvaged what I could, leaving behind
the compromised, giving to the tides
the rough drafts of a searching, struggling mind.
I built a shed of stone, a desk of light,
and wrote a sonnet on a laurel leaf,
and that's when it occurred to me to write
on, saying what I had to say in a sheaf
of sonnets. See this bottle? I've stuck them in
here and will send them out upon the ocean.